Chicken Wings

Cookbook

Introduction

Chicken wings are an American favorite! As a popular finger food they make great appetizers, are a favorite for a tailgate party, and they can even be a meal unto itself.

From hot and spicy to sweet and sticky, this recipe cookbook provides a range of styles to complement any meal or palate. If you are a serious connoisseur of the wing, you will want to try one or more of these great recipes!

Buffalo Chicken Hot Wings

Ingredients:

4 lbs. chicken wings, separated at joints, tips removed
Vegetable oil for frying
1 cup all-purpose flour
1/2 tsp. paprika
1/2 tsp. cayenne pepper
1/2 tsp. salt
1/2 cup butter
1/2 cup hot sauce
1/4 tsp. ground black pepper
1/4 tsp. garlic powder
Celery sticks.
Blue Cheese dressing for dipping

Directions:

1. In a small bowl mix together the flour, paprika, cayenne pepper and salt.
2. Place chicken wings in a large bowl and sprinkle flour mixture over them until they are evenly coated.
3. Cover dish or bowl and refrigerate for 60 to 90 minutes.
4. Heat oil in a large skillet.
5. Combine the butter, hot sauce, pepper and garlic powder in a small saucepan over low heat.
6. Stir together and heat until butter is melted and mixture is well blended.
7. Remove from heat and reserve for serving.
8. Fry coated wings in hot oil for 10 to 15 minutes, or until golden.
9. Remove from heat, place wings in serving bowl.
10. Add hot sauce mixture and stir together.
11. Serve with celery sticks and blue cheese dressing for dipping.

Five-Alarm Chicken Wings

Ingredients:

3 lbs. chicken wings, separated at joints, tips removed
Canola oil for frying
One 12-oz. bottle cayenne hot pepper sauce, such as
Frank's
1 stick butter
Several dashes Worcestershire sauce
As much hot sauce as you can stand. (such as Tabasco)
Blue cheese dip, for serving
Celery sticks and blue cheese dressing, for serving

Directions:

1. Preheat the oven to 325 degrees F. Heat 3 inches of canola oil in a heavy pot to 375 degrees F.
2. Add half the chicken wing parts to the oil and fry them until they're golden brown and fully cooked, 5 to 7 minutes.
3. Remove and drain on paper towels.
4. Repeat with the other half of the wing parts.
5. In a saucepan, heat the cayenne sauce and butter over medium-low heat.
6. Add the Worcestershire and hot sauce.
7. Let it bubble up, and then turn off the heat.
8. Place the wings in an ovenproof dish and pour the hot sauce over the top.
9. Toss to coat, and then bake in the oven for 15 minutes.
10. Serve with celery sticks and blue cheese dressing for dipping.

Japanese Chicken Wings

Ingredients:

3 lbs. chicken wings, separated at joints, tips discarded
1 egg, lightly beaten
1 cup all-purpose flour for coating
1 cup butter

Sauce Ingredients:

3 tbsps. soy sauce
3 tbsps. water
1 cup white sugar
1/2 cup white vinegar
1/2 tsp. garlic powder
1 tsp. salt

Directions:

1. Preheat oven to 350 degrees F (175 degrees C).
2. Dip wings in egg and coat with flour.
3. Heat butter in a large, deep skillet over medium-high heat.
4. Fry wings until deep brown.
5. Place in a shallow roasting pan.
6. In a small bowl combine soy sauce, water, sugar, vinegar, garlic powder and salt.
7. Pour over wings.
8. Bake in preheated oven for 30 to 45 minutes, basting wings often with sauce.

Garlic-Ginger Chicken Wings

Ingredients:

cooking spray
5 pounds chicken wings, separated at joints, tips removed
Salt and ground black pepper to taste
3 tbsps. hot sauce (such as Frank's Red Hot)
2 tbsps. vegetable oil
1 cup all-purpose flour
For the glaze:
3 crushed garlic cloves
2 tbsps. minced fresh ginger root
1 tbsp. Asian chile pepper sauce
1/2 cup rice vinegar
1/2 cup packed brown sugar
1 tbsp. soy sauce

Directions:

1. Preheat oven to 400 degrees F (200 degrees C).
2. Line 2 baking sheets with aluminum foil; grease the foil with cooking spray.
3. Place the chicken in a large mixing bowl.
4. Season with salt, pepper, and hot sauce.
5. Add the vegetable oil; toss to coat.
6. Place the flour and wings in a large, food-safe plastic bag. Hold the bag closed tightly, and shake to coat the wings entirely with the flour; no wet spots should remain.
7. Arrange the wings on the prepared baking sheets, making sure none of the pieces are touching one another. Spray wings with additional cooking spray
8. Bake in the preheated oven for 30 minutes, turn all the wings, and return to the oven to cook until crispy and no longer pink in the center, about 30 minutes more.
9. Whisk together the garlic, ginger, chili paste, rice vinegar, brown sugar, and soy sauce in a saucepan.
10. Bring the mixture to a boil and immediately remove from heat.

11. Put about half the wings in a large mixing bowl.
12. Pour about half the sauce over the wings.
13. Toss the wings with tongs to coat evenly; transfer to a tray and allow to sit about 5 minutes to allow the sauce to soak into the wings before serving.
14. Repeat with remaining wings and sauce.

Sweet Hot Mustard Chicken Wings

Ingredients:

2 lbs. chicken wings, separated at joints, tips removed
Salt to taste
2 tbsps. Dijon mustard
2 tbsps. prepared yellow mustard
3 tbsps. honey
2 tsps. cider vinegar
Salt and ground black pepper to taste
1 tsp. hot pepper sauce

Directions:

1. Preheat oven to 450 degrees F (230 degrees C).
2. Line a baking sheet with aluminum foil.
3. Coat the aluminum foil with cooking spray.
4. Arrange the wings on the prepared baking sheet so they do not touch.
5. Season with salt.
6. Bake in the preheated oven until browned and crispy on top, about 20 minutes.
7. Flip the wings with tongs and cook until no longer pink in the center and the juices run clear, about 20 minutes more.
8. Stir together the Dijon mustard, yellow mustard, honey, cider vinegar, salt, pepper, and hot sauce in large mixing bowl.
9. Add the wings to the bowl and toss with a spatula to coat evenly.
10. Allow to sit for about five minutes and toss again to re-coat.
11. Transfer to a plate to serve.

Mahogany Chicken Wings

Ingredients:

3 lbs. chicken wings, split and tips removed
1/2 cup soy sauce
1/2 cup honey
1/4 cup molasses
2 tbsps. chile sauce
1 tsp. ground ginger
2 cloves garlic, finely chopped

Directions:

1. Place chicken in a shallow, medium dish.
2. In a medium bowl, mix soy sauce, honey, molasses, chile sauce, ground ginger and garlic.
3. Pour the mixture over the chicken.
4. Cover and refrigerate approximately 1 hour, turning occasionally.
5. Preheat oven to 375 degrees F (190 degrees C).
6. In a large baking dish, arrange chicken in a single layer.
7. Bake in the preheated oven approximately 50 minutes, brushing with remaining soy sauce mixture often and turning once, until meat is no longer pink and juices run clear.

Honey Lime Chicken Wings

Ingredients:

18 whole chicken wings, split
1/4 cup honey
2 tbsps. fresh lime juice
1 tbsp. grated lime zest
1 clove garlic, minced
1/4 tsp. salt
1/4 tsp. ground black pepper
1/2 cup all-purpose flour
2 quarts vegetable oil for frying

Directions:

1. In a large bowl, mix together the honey, lime juice, lime peel, garlic, salt and ground black pepper.
2. Place the flour in a plastic bag and shake the chicken wings in the flour to coat.
3. In a large skillet, fry the chicken wings in hot, 1 inch deep oil until cooked through.
4. Place the cooked wings in the honey/lime mixture and toss to coat well.
5. Serve immediately.

Honey Sriracha Chicken Wings

Ingredients:

2 tbsps. baking powder
1 tbsp. kosher salt
1 tsp. freshly ground black pepper
1 tsp. smoked paprika
2 1/2 lbs. chicken wing sections

Honey Sriracha Glaze Ingredients:

1/3 cup honey
1/3 cup sriracha sauce
1 tbsp. seasoned rice vinegar
1/4 tsp. sesame oil
1 pinch sesame seeds, or as desired

Directions:

1. Preheat oven to 425 degrees F (220 degrees C).
2. Line a baking sheet with aluminum foil and place an oven-proof wire rack over the foil.
3. Whisk baking powder, salt, black pepper, and paprika together in a small bowl.
4. Place chicken wings in a large bowl.
5. Sprinkle 1/2 of the baking powder mixture over wings and toss to coat.
6. Sprinkle remaining baking powder mixture over wings and toss to coat again.
7. Place wings onto the rack of the prepared baking sheet.
8. Bake in the preheated oven for 20 minutes.
9. Turn wings and continue baking for 20 minutes.
10. Turn wings again and bake until wings are browned and crispy, about 15 minutes more.
11. Transfer wings to a large bowl.
12. Whisk honey, sriracha sauce, rice vinegar, and sesame oil together in a bowl until glaze is smooth.
13. Drizzle glaze over wings and toss to coat completely.

14. Transfer wings to a serving platter and sprinkle sesame seeds over the top.

Balinese Chicken Wings

Ingredients:

4 cloves garlic, minced
1 fresh red chile pepper, finely chopped
1 shallot, minced
1 (1 inch) piece fresh turmeric root, peeled and minced
1 tsp. kosher salt
1 tbsp. brown sugar
2 tsps. olive oil
12 chicken wings, separated at joints, tips removed

Directions:

1. Combine garlic, chile pepper, shallot, turmeric, and kosher salt; bruise with a mortar and pestle, or with the flat side of a cleaver.
2. Place into a bowl, and stir in brown sugar, and olive oil.
3. Toss chicken wings with marinade, cover, and refrigerate for at least 1 hour.
4. Preheat oven to 400 degrees F (200 degrees C).
5. Line a baking sheet with aluminum foil.
6. Toss the chicken wings again to recoat in marinade, then spread out onto prepared baking sheet.
7. Bake in preheated oven until deep, golden brown, about 30 minutes.

Alfredo Chicken Wings

Ingredients:

3 lbs. chicken wings
1 tbsp. seasoned salt
1/4 cup salted butter
1 cup heavy cream
1 tbsp. minced garlic
1 1/4 cups grated Parmesan cheese

Directions:

1. Preheat oven to 375 degrees F (190 degrees C).
2. Grease a large rimmed baking sheet.
3. Place wings on prepared baking sheet.
4. Sprinkle with seasoned salt; mix to evenly season the wings.
5. Arrange in a single layer.
6. Bake in preheated oven until crisp and cooked through, about 1 hour.
7. Turn on oven broiler.
8. Finish the wings under the broiler to crisp both sides, about 1 minute per side.
9. Melt butter over medium-low heat in a small saucepan.
10. Add cream and garlic stirring until small bubbles form.
11. Add grated cheese and continue to stir until well blended.
12. Remove pan from heat.
13. Toss wings with Alfredo sauce and serve.

Sesame Chicken Wings

Ingredients:

2 lbs. chicken wings
1/2 cup honey
2/3 cup prepared mustard
1/2 lemon, juiced
1 tsp. curry powder
3 cloves crushed garlic
Ground black pepper to taste
1/2 cup sesame seeds

Directions:

1. Combine honey, mustard , lemon juice, curry powder, garlic, and pepper in a resealable plastic bag.
2. Add chicken wings, and marinate at least 1 hour in refrigerator.
3. Meanwhile, toast sesame seeds by placing on a cookie sheet in a 350 degree F (175 degrees C) oven for approximately 10 to 15 minutes, shaking to toss occasionally.
4. Remove wings from marinade.
5. Broil for 5 to 10 minutes on each side, or until well cooked.
6. Baste with marinade every few minutes.
7. Remove from oven, and sprinkle liberally with the sesame seeds.

Pacific Chicken Wings

Ingredients:

3 lbs. chicken wings
1 cup soy sauce
1 cup packed brown sugar
1/2 cup butter
1 tsp. mustard powder
3/4 cup water

Directions:

1. Disjoint the chicken wings, discarding the tips.
2. Combine the soy sauce, brown sugar, butter or margarine, mustard and water and heat until the sugar and butter dissolve.
3. Let mixture cool and pour over wings.
4. Marinate in the refrigerator for 2 hours, turning occasionally.
5. Preheat oven to 350 degrees F (175 degrees C).
6. Bake chicken wings in marinade for 45 minutes, turning once and spooning marinade over chicken occasionally.
7. Drain on paper towels and serve.

BBQ Chicken Wings

Ingredients:

5 pounds chicken wings, cut into sections, tips removed
2 1/2 cups hot and spicy ketchup
2/3 cup white vinegar
1/2 cup honey
2 tbsps. honey 1/2 cup molasses
1 tsp. salt
1 tsp. Worcestershire sauce
1/2 tsp. onion powder
1/2 tsp. chili powder
1/2 tsp. liquid smoke

Directions:

1. Preheat oven to 375 degrees F (190 degrees C).
2. Grease two 15x10x1-inch baking pans.
3. Arrange chicken in the prepared baking pans.
4. Bake in the preheated oven for 30 minutes; drain and turn wings. Continue baking until no longer pink in the center and juices run clear, 20 to 25 minutes.
5. An instant-read thermometer inserted near the bone should read 165 degrees F (74 degrees C).
6. Drain.
7. Combine ketchup, vinegar, 1/2 cup and 2 tbsps. honey, molasses, salt, Worcestershire sauce, onion powder, chili powder, and liquid smoke in a large saucepan; bring to a boil.
8. Reduce heat and simmer until sauce has thickened and flavors blended, 25 to 30 minutes.
9. Transfer 1/3 the chicken to a slow cooker and top with about 1 cup sauce.
10. Repeat layering with remaining chicken and sauce.
11. Cook on Low, 3 to 4 hours.
12. Stir before serving.

Lemon Dijon Chicken Wings

Ingredients:

2 lbs. chicken wings, separated at joints, tips removed
1/4 cup olive oil
1 tbsp. fresh lemon juice
2 tbsps. coarse-grained Dijon mustard
6 cloves garlic, chopped
2 tsps. salt
1 tbsp. freshly ground black pepper

Directions:

1. In a large bowl, stir together the olive oil, lemon juice, mustard, garlic, salt, and pepper.
2. Add chicken wings, cover, and marinate in the refrigerator for at least 2 hours, stirring occasionally.
3. Preheat grill for high heat.
4. Drain marinade from chicken into a small saucepan.
5. Bring to a boil, and simmer for 5 minutes.
6. Set aside for basting.
7. Lightly oil the grill grate.
8. Grill wings for 10 to 15 minutes, or until juices run clear.
9. Turn frequently and baste with the marinade during the last 5 minutes.

Lemon Pepper Chicken Wings

Ingredients:

6 tbsps. olive oil
1/4 cup finely grated lemon zest
2 tbsps. coarse sea salt
2 tbsps. ground black pepper
1 (3 pound) bag chicken wings

Directions:

1. Preheat oven to 425 degrees F (220 degrees C).
2. Line a baking sheet with parchment paper.
3. Whisk olive oil, lemon zest, salt, and black pepper together in a bowl; add wings and toss to coat.
4. Spread coated wings in a single layer onto the prepared baking sheet.
5. Bake in the preheated oven until no longer pink at the bone and the juices run clear, about 35 minutes.
6. An instant-read thermometer inserted near the bone should read 165 degrees F (74 degrees C).
7. Bake longer for a crispier skin.

Bombay Chicken Wings

Ingredients:

24 chicken wings
2 tbsps. vegetable oil
2 tbsps. soy sauce
2 tbsps. minced green onion
2 cloves garlic, minced
1 tsp. curry powder
1/2 tsp. ground turmeric
1/8 tsp. ground black pepper

Directions:

1. Combine chicken wings, vegetable oil, soy sauce, green onion, garlic, curry powder, turmeric, and black pepper in a resealable plastic bag.
2. Squeeze out the air, seal bag, and refrigerate at least 1 hour.
3. Preheat oven to 350 degrees F (175 degrees C).
4. Spread chicken wings into a large baking dish.
5. Bake in the preheated oven until wings are browned, about 25 minutes.

Pastrami Chicken Wings

Ingredients:

2 1/2 lbs. chicken wings, separated at joints, tips removed
1 tbsp. vegetable oil
1/4 tsp. white pepper
1 tbsp. freshly ground black pepper
1 1/2 tbsps. Ground coriander
1 tbsp. smoked paprika
1 pinch cayenne pepper (optional)
2 tsps. Kosher salt
2 tsps. All-purpose flour

Directions:

1. Preheat oven to 425 degrees F (220 degrees C).
2. Line a baking sheet with parchment paper or a silicon mat.
3. Combine the chicken wings, vegetable oil, white pepper, black pepper, coriander, paprika, cayenne pepper, and salt in a large mixing bowl; toss with a spatula to coat evenly.
4. Sprinkle with flour; toss again to coat evenly.
5. Bake in the preheated oven until browned on top, about 25 minutes. Turn the wings and return to oven to bake until crisp, no longer pink in the center, and the juices run clear, about 20 minutes more.
6. Remove immediately to a serving dish.

Teriyaki Chicken Wings

Ingredients:

3 lbs. chicken wings, separated at joints, tips removed
1 cup water
1 cup soy sauce
1 cup white sugar
1/4 cup pineapple juice
1/4 cup vegetable oil
1 tbsp. minced fresh garlic
1 tbsp. minced fresh ginger

Directions:

1. Whisk together the water, soy sauce, sugar, pineapple juice, vegetable oil, garlic, and ginger in a large glass or ceramic bowl until the sugar has dissolved.
2. Add the chicken wings, coat with the marinade, cover the bowl with plastic wrap, and marinate in the refrigerator for at least 1 hour.
3. Preheat an oven to 350 degrees F (175 degrees C).
4. Grease baking dishes, and set aside.
5. Remove the chicken from the marinade, and shake off excess and place the chicken wings into the prepared baking dishes.
6. Discard the remaining marinade.
7. Bake the wings in the preheated oven until the chicken is cooked through and the glaze is evenly browned, about 1 hour.

Chinese Barbecue Chicken Wings

Ingredients:

3 lbs. chicken wings, separated at joints, tips removed
Cooking spray
1/2 cup hoisin sauce
1/3 cup low sodium teriyaki sauce
1/4 cup brown sugar
2 cloves garlic, minced
1 tbsp. grated fresh ginger
1 tbsp. chile-garlic sauce, or to taste

Directions:

1. Preheat the oven to 375 degrees F (190 degrees C).
2. Spray a baking sheet with cooking spray.
3. Whisk together hoisin sauce, teriyaki sauce, brown sugar, garlic, ginger, and chili-garlic sauce in a bowl.
4. Arrange chicken wing pieces on the prepared baking sheet.
5. Brush chicken with hoisin sauce mixture.
6. Bake in the preheated oven until chicken wings are no longer pink in the center, 20 to 25 minutes on each side, basting every 15 minutes.

Cola Chicken Wings

Ingredients:

4 lbs. chicken wings, separated at joints, tips removed
1 tsp. garlic salt
1 tsp. onion powder
1 (12 fluid oz.) can cola-flavored carbonated beverage
1 cup packed light brown sugar
2 tbsps. soy sauce

Directions:

1. Preheat oven to 325 degrees F (165 degrees C).
2. Place chicken wings in a shallow casserole dish.
3. Season with garlic salt and onion salt.
4. Mix cola, sugar, and soy sauce; pour mixture over chicken wings.
5. Bake, covered, at 325 degrees F (165 degrees C) for 2 hours.
6. Turn wings over every 30 minutes.
7. Uncover, and bake for an additional 1 to 2 hours.
8. Turn wings every 30 minutes or so.

Peanut Sate Chicken Wings

Ingredients:

3 lbs. chicken wings, separated at joints, tips removed
1 cup water
1/2 cup white sugar
1/3 cup soy sauce
2 tbsps. peanut butter
1 tbsp. honey
2 tsps. wine vinegar
1 tbsp. minced garlic

1 tsp. sesame seeds, or to taste

Directions:

1. In an electric skillet or a large skillet over medium heat, mix together the water, sugar, soy sauce, peanut butter, honey, wine vinegar, and garlic until smooth and the sugar has dissolved.
2. Place the wings into the sauce, cover, and simmer for 30 minutes.
3. Uncover and simmer until the wings are tender and the sauce has thickened, about 30 more minutes, spooning sauce over wings occasionally.
4. Sprinkle with sesame seeds.

Jamaican Jerk Chicken Wings

Ingredients:

3 lbs. chicken wings, separated at joints, tips removed
1/4 cup fresh squeezed orange juice
2 tbsps. lemon juice
2 tbsps. lime juice
1 tsp. salt
2 tsps. ground black pepper
1 tbsp. chopped fresh thyme
1 tbsp. chopped garlic
1 tbsp. chopped fresh ginger
1 habanero pepper, seeded and chopped
1 tbsp. curry powder
1/2 tsp. ground allspice
1/4 tsp. ground nutmeg
1/4 tsp. ground cinnamon
1/2 cup vegetable oil

Directions:

1. Mix together the orange juice, lemon juice, lime juice, salt, black pepper, thyme, garlic, ginger, habanero pepper, curry powder, allspice, nutmeg, and cinnamon in a bowl. Whisk in the vegetable oil.
2. Pour 3/4 of the marinade into a resealable plastic zipper bag, and place the chicken wing pieces into the bag.
3. Squeeze out any air, and mix the wing pieces with the marinade, and refrigerate from 4 to 12 hours.
4. Place the remaining 1/4 of the marinade in a small bowl, and refrigerate until grilling time.
5. Preheat an outdoor grill for medium heat, and lightly oil the grate.
6. Remove the wing pieces from the bag of marinade, and discard the used marinade.
7. Sprinkle the wings with salt and pepper to taste, and sear on the hottest part of the grill until the wings begin to brown, about 4 minutes per side.

8. Move the wings to a less-hot part of the grill, baste with the unused portion of the marinade, and close the grill.
9. Grill until the wings are golden brown, show good grill marks, are no longer pink in the center, and the juices run clear, 10 to 15 more minutes.
10. Baste again with marinade and turn after 5 to 8 minutes.

Maple Bourbon Chipotle Chicken Wings

Ingredients:

3 lbs. chicken wings, separated at joints, tips removed

Spice Rub Ingredients:

2 tsp olive oil to coat wings
1/8 tsp. sea salt
1/8 tsp. black pepper
1/8 tsp. chipotle powder
1/2 tsp. garlic powder
1 tsp. smoked paprika
1 1/2 tsps. maple sugar

Sauce Ingredients:

6 slices of bacon (cut into 1 inch pieces)
4 cloves minced garlic
1 tbsp. grated shallot
2 tsps. chipotle chilies minced (from can of chipotles in adobo sauce)
1 tbsp. cider vinegar
2 tbsps. tomato paste
1/4 cup bourbon
1/2 cup maple syrup

Directions:

1. Preheat oven to 350 degrees F.
2. Place chicken wings in a large bowl and drizzle with oil to coat.
3. Whisk together all dry ingredients from spice rub in a small bowl.
4. Add spice rub to chicken, using your hands to coat wings evenly.
5. Let rest for 15-20 minutes.
6. Prepare a pan for the oven by lining with foil (for easy clean-up), and placing a wire rack in the pan.

7. Place chicken wings skin side down in single layer on rack, and bake for 40 minutes in center of oven, turning wings over after 20 minutes.
8. Turn over once more and broil for 4-5 minutes for crispy skin.
9. While wings are baking, prepare the sauce.
10. Cook bacon in a sauce pan over medium heat until lightly browned then remove from pan.
11. Add garlic and shallots to pan and cook for 2 minutes or until softened.
12. Add chilies and cook for 2 more minutes.
13. Add remaining sauce ingredients and return bacon to the pan.
14. Bring to a boil, then turn heat down to a simmer for 15 minutes to combine the flavors. Set aside.
15. When wings are done, cover with sauce and provide extra sauce for dipping.

Supreme Buffalo Wings

Wings Ingredients:

3 lbs. chicken wings, separated at joints, tips removed
Flour for dredging
Vegetable oil for frying
6 tbsps. butter, melted
2 tbsps. celery leaves
1 cup crumbled blue cheese

Sauce Ingredients:

2/3 cup hot pepper sauce (such as Frank's Red Hot)
1/2 cup cold unsalted butter
1 1/2 tbsps. white vinegar
1/4 tsp. Worcestershire sauce
1/4 tsp. cayenne pepper
1/8 tsp. garlic powder
1/2 tsp. celery salt
Salt to taste

Directions:

1. Heat oil in a frying pan to 375 degrees F.
2. Working in batches, deep-fry the chicken wings until golden, about 15 minutes.
3. Drain on paper towels.
4. Combine the hot sauce, 6 tbsps. butter, celery salt, vinegar, Worcestershire sauce, cayenne pepper, garlic powder, and salt in a pot and place over medium heat.
5. Bring to a simmer while stirring with a whisk.
6. As soon as the liquid begins to bubble on the sides of the pot, remove from heat.
7. Stir again with the whisk.
8. Toss the cooked chicken wings with 6 tbsps. butter, celery leaves, blue cheese and wing sauce.
9. Serve with celery sticks and blue cheese dressing and enjoy!

Moroccan Chicken Wings

Ingredients:

4 lbs. chicken wings, separated at joints, tips removed
1 tbsp. ground cinnamon
2 tsps. cracked black pepper
3/4 tsp. ground coriander
1/2 tsp. ground cumin
1/2 tsp. ground cloves
1/2 tsp. ground cardamom
2 tbsps. paprika
4 garlic cloves, pressed (or mashed)
2 tbsps. dark brown sugar
1 tsp. salt
1 tsp. red pepper flakes
2 tbsps. olive oil
2 tbsps. fresh lemon juice

Dipping Sauce Ingredients:

1 cup Greek yogurt
2 tbsps. olive oil
2 tbsps. chopped mint

Directions:

1. For the marinade, toast cinnamon, pepper, coriander, cumin, cloves and cardamom in skillet over medium-high heat until very fragrant, 2 to 3 minutes; cool.
2. Transfer to small bowl.
3. Stir in paprika, garlic, sugar, salt, pepper flakes, oil, juice.
4. Cut wing tips off chicken; halve wings at joint.
5. Combine wings with marinade in plastic bag.
6. Chill in refrigerator 45 minutes.
7. Heat oven to 450 degrees F.
8. Spread wings in large rimmed baking sheet.
9. Bake in oven 25 minutes, turning occasionally. Increase heat to broil.

10. Cook wings under broiler 10 minutes or until skin is crisp.
11. Mix together dipping sauce ingredients.
12. Serve wings with dipping sauce and enjoy!

Vietnamese Chicken Wings

4 lbs. chicken wings, separated at joints, tips removed
1/2 cup chicken bouillon powder
1/2 cup Vietnamese chili sauce
1/2 cup honey
1/2 cup cooking oil
1/2 cup pureed shallot
1/4 cup rice vinegar
20 kaffir lime leaves, finely chopped
1 cup cilantro leaves
1 cup roasted peanuts, chopped

Directions:

1. Combine the bouillon, chili sauce, honey, oil, shallots, vinegar and lime leaves and whisk together to form a uniform paste.
2. Reserve some paste for brushing, and place the rest in a resealable plastic bag.
3. Toss the chicken wings in the paste in the bag and allow to marinate for 30 minutes to 1 hour.
4. Build a hot charcoal fire on one side of the grill.
5. Set the chicken wings on the grill opposite of the hot coal side.
6. Cover the grill and cook until the wings are just about cooked through, 25 to 30 minutes.
7. Rotate the wings halfway through for even cooking.
8. To finish the wings, brush with the reserved paste and grill directly over hot coals until charred slightly.
9. Transfer to a platter and top with cilantro leaves and peanuts.

Beer-Battered Chicken Wings

Ingredients:

4 lbs. chicken wings, separated at joints, tips removed
1 large egg
3/4 cup beer
1 cup all purpose flour
1 tsp. baking soda
1 tsp. salt
1/2 tsp. ground black pepper
1/2 tsp. ground cayenne pepper
1/2 tsp. garlic salt
canola oil
Malt vinegar, for dipping

Directions:

1. Whisk the egg in a medium bowl, then slowly adding the beer to the egg mixture.
2. Whisk together until combined well.
3. In a separate small mixing bowl add the flour, baking soda and seasonings.
4. Slowly add the dry mixture into the egg and beer mixture.
5. Mix well and let sit for at least 30 minutes.
6. While the batter sits, bring a large pot of salty water to a boil, then add the wings.
7. Boil for about 5 minutes, just until chicken begins to look like it's cooking and is no longer raw.
8. Remove the chicken from the water and pat completely dry. Submerge the wing in the beer batter, you can add a few at a time.
9. Be sure both sides are coated well.
10. Add oil to deep fryer and bring temperature up to 375.
11. Add a handful of wings at a time to the fryer, being sure to shake the chicken around a bit to get an even fry.
12. Once they are golden brown and the coating is crisp, they can be removed.

13. Place them on a plate lined with paper towels until you have fried all of the chicken batches.
14. Serve with malt vinegar.
15. Serve with celery sticks and blue cheese dressing and enjoy!

Buttermilk Chicken Wings

Ingredients:

4 lbs. chicken wings, separated at joints, tips removed
1 1/2 cups buttermilk
1/2 tsp. kosher salt
1 1/2 cups flour
1 tsp. paprika
1/2 tsp. kosher salt
Vegetable oil for frying

Directions:

1. Mix buttermilk with kosher salt.
2. Soak the wings in buttermilk mixture, 30 minutes.
3. In a separate bowl, mix together flour, paprika and kosher salt.
4. Drain the wings.
5. Dredge the wings in the flour mixture.
6. Deep-fry in heated oil until dark golden, about 10 minutes.
7. Serve with celery sticks and blue cheese dressing and enjoy!

Cajun Buttermilk Chicken Wings

Ingredients:

4 lbs. chicken wings, separated at joints, tips removed
1 1/2 cups buttermilk
1/2 tsp. kosher salt
1 1/2 cups flour
1 tsp. paprika
1/2 tsp. kosher salt
1/4 cup hot sauce
2 tbsps. Cajun seasoning
Vegetable oil for frying

Directions:

1. Mix buttermilk with kosher salt.
2. Soak the wings in buttermilk mixture, 30 minutes.
3. In a separate bowl, mix together flour, paprika and kosher salt.
4. Drain the wings.
5. Dredge the wings in the flour mixture.
6. Deep-fry in heated oil until dark golden, about 10 minutes.
7. Serve with celery sticks and blue cheese dressing and enjoy!

Chili Chicken Wings

Ingredients:

3 lbs. chicken wings, split at the joints, tips removed
Vegetable oil for frying
1/2 cup cornstarch
1/2 tsp. salt
To Make the Sauce
1/2 cup rice vinegar
1 1/2 cups water
2/3 cup sugar
1 tsp. salt
3 cloves garlic finely minced
1 1/2 tbsps. chili paste
2 tbsps. cornstarch mixed with 3 tbsps. water to make a slurry

Directions:

1. Heat about 2 inches of vegetable oil in a large deep skillet or use a deep fat fryer.
2. Mix the cornstarch with the salt in a shallow dish and coat the chicken with the mixture.
3. Shake off any excess.
4. Fry the chicken wings in the hot oil until the exterior is golden brown and crispy and they are cooked through on the inside, about 12 minutes. Turn a few times to ensure even cooking and avoid burning.
5. Once all the wings are ready, mix all sauce ingredients except for the chili paste and the cornstarch slurry in a large frying pan.
6. Bring to the boil and cook until slightly thickened, about 3-4 minutes.
7. Stir in the chili paste and bring to the boil again.
8. Stir in the cornstarch slurry and continue cooking until thickened, about 1-2 minutes.
9. Add the chicken wings to the sauce, toss until coated and cook over low heat until heated through. Serve immediately.

Maryland Chicken Wings

Ingredients:

3 lbs. chicken wings, separated at joints, tips removed
1/4 cup flour
2 tbsps. Old Bay Seasoning
1/4 cup butter, melted
1/4 cup hot sauce
Blue cheese dressing and celery sticks (optional)

Grilling Directions:

1. Mix flour and OLD BAY in large resealable plastic bag.
2. Add chicken wings in batches; shake to coat well.
3. Grill over medium-high heat 20 to 25 minutes or until chicken is cooked through and skin is crisp, turning frequently.
4. Meanwhile, mix butter and hot sauce in large bowl.
5. Add cooked wings.
6. Toss to coat.
7. Serve wings with blue cheese dressing and celery sticks.

Baking Directions:

1. Preheat oven to 450 degrees F.
2. Coat wings as directed.
3. Arrange in single layer on foil-lined 15x10x1-inch baking pan sprayed with no stick cooking spray.
4. Bake 30 to 45 minutes or until chicken is cooked through and skin is crisp.
5. Serve wings with blue cheese dressing and celery sticks.

Italian Chicken Wings

Ingredients:

3 lbs. chicken wings, separated at joints, tips removed
3/4 cup Italian breadcrumbs
Flour for dredging.
3/4 cup grated Parmesan
1/4 cup chopped parsley
3 eggs, beaten

Directions:

1. Mix Italian breadcrumbs, grated Parmesan and chopped parsley in a small bowl.
2. Beat eggs in a separate bowl.
3. Dredge the wings in flour, then dip in eggs and then coat in the breadcrumb mixture.
4. Deep-fry in 350 degrees F oil until crisp and golden, about 12 minutes.

Chicken Wings Parmesan

Ingredients:

3 lbs. chicken wings, split at the joints, tips removed
3/4 cup Italian breadcrumbs
Flour for dredging.
3/4 cup grated Parmesan
1/4 cup chopped parsley
3 eggs, beaten
Marinara sauce as needed
Grated mozzarella cheese
Grated Parmesan cheese

Directions:

1. Mix Italian breadcrumbs, grated Parmesan and chopped parsley in a small bowl.
2. Beat eggs in a separate bowl.
3. Dredge the wings in flour, then dip in eggs and then coat in the breadcrumb mixture.
4. Deep-fry in 350 degrees F oil until crisp and golden, about 12 minutes.
5. Top with marinara sauce, then mozzarella and Parmesan.
6. Heat oven to broil.
7. Broil until the cheese melts
8. Serve with warm marinara sauce.

Ancho Peach Chicken Wings

Ingredients:

3 lbs. chicken wings, split at the joints, tips removed
Flour for dredging
Vegetable oil for frying
1/2 cup peach preserves
1 1/2 tbsps. lemon juice
1 1/2 tbsps. soy sauce
1 tsp. ancho chile powder

Directions:

1. Heat oil in a pan.
2. Dredge the wings in flour and deep-fry until golden brown and crispy.
3. Drain on paper towels.
4. Mix together peach preserves, lemon juice and soy sauce, and ancho chile powder in a large bowl.
5. Toss the wings in the mixture to coat.
6. Serve and enjoy!

Asian Honey Chicken Wings

Ingredients:

3 lbs. chicken wings, split at the joints, tips removed
Flour for dredging
6 tbsps. butter, melted
1/4 cup honey
2 tbsps. soy sauce

Directions:

1. Dredge the wings in flour.
2. Deep-fry in vegetable oil.
3. Drain on paper towels.
4. Mix together butter, honey and soy sauce.
5. Toss with wings and enjoy!

Pecan Sesame Chicken Wings

Ingredients:

3 lbs. chicken wings, split at the joints, tips removed
Vegetable oil for frying
1/3 cup sesame seeds
1/3 cup pecans
2 cups breadcrumbs
2 tbsps. chives, finely chopped
Kosher salt, and black pepper to taste
3 eggs
Honey mustard for dipping

Directions:

1. Grind up sesame seeds and pecans in a food processor.
2. Stir together in a bowl sesame pecan mix with breadcrumbs, chives, salt and pepper.
3. Beat eggs in a separate bowl.
4. Dip wings first in eggs and then in breadcrumb mixture.
5. Fry in heated oil until golden, 12 minutes.
6. Drain on paper towels.
7. Serve with honey mustard for dipping.

Falafel Chicken Wings

Ingredients:

3 lbs. chicken wings, split at the joints, tips removed
2 1/2 cups dry falafel mix, divided
3 eggs
1/4 cup chopped parsley

Directions:

1. Beat eggs in a shallow bowl.
2. Put 1 cup falafel mix in another bowl.
3. Mix 1 1/2 cups of falafel mix with parsley in a third bowl.
4. Heat oil in a pan.
5. Dredge the wings in first falafel mix plain, then eggs, then falafel and parsley mix.
6. Fry in heated oil until golden, 10 minutes.
7. Drain on paper towels.

Curry Chutney Chicken Wings

Ingredients:

3 lbs. chicken wings, split at the joints, tips removed
Flour for dredging
Vegetable oil for frying
1/3 cup lime juice
1/3 cup mango chutney
1 red jalapeno, chopped
6 tbsps. butter, melted
2 tsps. fresh cilantro, chopped
2 tsps. curry powder

Directions:

1. Heat oil in a pan.
2. Dredge the wings in flour. and then deep-fry.
3. Drain on paper towels.
4. Pulse together in a food processor the chutney, lime juice, jalapeno, butter and curry powder.
5. Toss mixture with the wings.
6. Sprinkle with cilantro.

Chipotle Chicken Wings

Ingredients:

3 lbs. chicken wings, split at the joints, tips removed
Flour for dredging
Vegetable oil for frying
3 tbsps. chopped chipotle chiles in adobo sauce
1/4 cup honey
1/4 cup cider vinegar
3 tbsps. melted butter
1/2 tsp. ground cumin

Directions:

1. Dredge the wings in flour.
2. Deep-fry in heated oil.
3. In a food processor, purée together chiles, vinegar, honey, butter and cumin.
4. Toss with the wings and enjoy!

Korean Kimchi Chicken Wings

Ingredients:

2 lbs. chicken wings, split at the joints, tips removed
3 tbsps. gochujang (Korean hot-pepper paste)
2 tbsps. rice vinegar
2 tbsps. honey
1 tsp. sesame oil
3 tbsps. gochugaru (Korean hot-pepper powder)
1 tbsp. roasted sesame seeds, plus more for garnish
Vegetable oil (for frying)
Salt and pepper, to taste
1 tbsp. flour (plus more if necessary), for dredging
1 tbsp. cornstarch (plus more if necessary), for dredging

Directions:

1. Lay wings in a single layer on a wax paper-lined baking sheet, and place in the refrigerator (uncovered) for one hour.
2. Whisk together the red-pepper paste, rice vinegar, honey, sesame oil, red-pepper powder, and sesame seeds in a large bowl.
3. Heat vegetable oil in a Dutch oven over medium heat.
4. Remove wings from refrigerator and season on all sides with salt and pepper.
5. Place about a tbsp. each of flour and cornstarch in a large clean plastic bag, seal, and shake gently to combine.
6. Working in batches, drop a few chicken wings in the bag, and toss to coat with the flour mixture.
7. Shake off the excess before dropping each wing into the hot oil, and fry until golden brown, turning occasionally, about five to seven minutes.
8. Replenish the flour mixture in the bag as needed.
9. Transfer fried wings to a wire rack placed over a rimmed baking sheet.
10. When wings are cooled slightly but still warm, toss them in the sauce and pile them on a serving platter.

11. Garnish with more sesame seeds and serve!

Steakhouse Chicken Wings

Ingredients:

3 lbs. chicken wings, split at the joints, tips removed
2 tbsps. coarsely ground pepper
1/3 cup steak sauce
Salt to taste

Directions:

1. Heat oven to 425 degrees F.
2. Grease two rimmed baking sheets.
3. Toss wings with pepper and salt to taste.
4. Spread wings in a single layer on the baking sheets.
5. Roast wings until very crisp, about 45 minutes.
6. Mix wings with steak sauce.
7. Serve and enjoy!

Rosemary-Lemon Chicken Wings

Ingredients:

3 lbs. chicken wings, split at the joints, tips removed
1/4 cup lemon-pepper seasoning
2 tsps. chopped rosemary

Directions:

1. Preheat oven to 425 degrees F.
2. Grease two rimmed baking sheets.
3. Toss the wings with lemon-pepper seasoning and chopped rosemary.
4. Spread wings in a single layer on the baking sheets.
5. Roast wings until very crisp, about 45 minutes.
6. Serve and enjoy!

Horseradish-Crusted Chicken Wings

Ingredients:

3 lbs. chicken wings, split at the joints, tips removed
1/2 cup dijon mustard
1/4 cup horseradish
1 1/2 cups panko breadcrumbs
1/2 cup grated Parmesan
1 tsp. paprika

Directions:

1. Preheat oven to 425 degrees F.
2. Grease two rimmed baking sheets.
3. Mix Dijon mustard and horseradish together in a small bowl.
4. Pour over wings and toss to coat.
5. Toss the wings with 1/2 cup Dijon mustard and 1/4 cup horseradish.
6. In a small bowl, mix together breadcrumbs, Parmesan and paprika.
7. Sprinkle breadcrumb mixture over the wings and toss to coat.
8. Spread wings in a single layer on the baking sheets.
9. Roast until browned, about 35 minutes.
10. Serve and enjoy!

Maple-Bacon Chicken Wings

Ingredients:

3 lbs. chicken wings, split at the joints, tips removed
8 slices bacon
1 tbsp. bacon drippings
Salt and pepper to taste
1/4 cup maple syrup
2 tbsps. cider vinegar
2 tbsps. bourbon

Directions:

1. Preheat oven to 425 degrees F.
2. Grease two rimmed baking sheets.
3. Fry bacon in a skillet until crisp.
4. Drain bacon and crumble, reserving 1 tbsp. of the drippings.
5. Season the wings with salt and pepper.
6. Spread in a single layer on the baking sheets.
7. Roast for 35 minutes until brown.
8. Whisk together bacon drippings, maple syrup, vinegar and bourbon.
9. Toss the wings with the syrup mixture and bacon.
10. Serve and enjoy!

Mango Barbecue Chicken Wings

Ingredients:

3 lbs. chicken wings, split at the joints, tips removed
Salt and pepper to taste
1 cup mango nectar
3 tbsps. barbecue sauce

Directions:

1. Preheat oven to 425 degrees F.
2. Grease two rimmed baking sheets.
3. Season the wings with salt and pepper.
4. Spread wings in a single layer on the baking sheets.
5. Roast wings until very crisp, about 45 minutes.
6. In a pot, simmer mango nectar and barbecue sauce until reduced to 1/2 cup, about 20 minutes.
7. Toss with the wings.
8. Serve and enjoy!

Teriyaki Orange Chicken Wings

Ingredients:

3 lbs. chicken wings, split at the joints, tips removed
3/4 cup orange juice and
1/4 cup teriyaki
Salt and pepper to taste

Directions:

1. Preheat oven to 425 degrees F.
2. Grease two rimmed baking sheets.
3. Season the wings with salt and pepper.
4. Spread wings in a single layer on the baking sheets.
5. Roast wings until very crisp, about 45 minutes.
6. In a medium pot, simmer orange juice and teriyaki sauce until reduced by half, about 15 minutes.
7. Toss with the wings.
8. Serve and enjoy!

Honey Mustard Chicken Wings

Ingredients:

3 lbs. chicken wings, split at the joints, tips removed
1 tbsp. butter, melted
1/3 cup Dijon mustard
1/4 cup honey
Paprika to taste
Salt and pepper to taste

Directions:

1. Preheat oven to 425 degrees F.
2. Grease two rimmed baking sheets.
3. Season the wings with salt and pepper.
4. Spread wings in a single layer on the baking sheets.
5. Roast wings until very crisp, about 45 minutes.
6. Whisk butter with Dijon mustard and honey.
7. Toss mixture with the wings.
8. Sprinkle with paprika.
9. Serve and enjoy!

Honey Mustard Pretzel Chicken Wings

Ingredients:

3 lbs. chicken wings, split at the joints, tips removed
1/2 cup honey mustard plus more for dipping
1/2 tsp. kosher salt
1/2 tsp. pepper
4 cups pretzels

Directions:

1. Preheat oven to 425 degrees F.
2. Toss the wings with 1/2 cup honey mustard and kosher salt and pepper.
3. Grind pretzels in a food processor.
4. Transfer ground pretzels to a bowl.
5. Add the wings and toss to coat.
6. Roast until crisp, about 40 minutes.
7. Serve with honey mustard for dipping.
8. Enjoy!

Ginger Scallion Chicken Wings

Ingredients:

3 lbs. chicken wings, split at the joints, tips removed
1/2 cup minced scallions
2 tbsps. butter
2 tbsps. grated ginger
2 tbsps. grated soy sauce
2 tbsps. grated mirin (or sake)
3/4 tsp. kosher salt
3/4 tsp. sesame oil

Directions:

1. Roast the wings.
2. Preheat oven to 425 degrees F.
3. Grease two rimmed baking sheets.
4. Season the wings with salt and pepper.
5. Spread wings in a single layer on the baking sheets.
6. Roast wings until very crisp, about 45 minutes.
7. In a saucepan, heat all ingredients except for the wings.
8. Toss with the wings.
9. Serve and enjoy!

Thai Chili Chicken Wings

Ingredients:

3 lbs. chicken wings, split at the joints, tips removed
1 cup Thai sweet chili sauce
1 Carrot, shredded
2 tbsps. olive oil
2 tbsps. lime juice
2 tbsps. grated ginger
2 tsps. kosher salt
Lime wedges for serving

Directions:

1. In a large bowl, mix together the Thai sweet chili sauce, carrot, olive oil, lime juice, grated ginger, and kosher salt.
2. Marinate the wings for 2 hours in the mixture.
3. Drain, reserving the marinade.
4. Preheat the oven to 475 degrees F.
5. Grease two rimmed baking sheets.
6. Spread wings in a single layer on the baking sheets.
7. Roast for 15 minutes.
8. Brush with the marinade and roast until slightly charred, 25 more minutes.
9. Serve with lime wedges.

Taco Flavored Chicken Wings

Ingredients:

3 lbs. chicken wings, split at the joints, tips removed
3 tbsps. taco seasoning
Salsa for dipping

Directions:

1. Toss the wings with the taco seasoning.
2. Preheat oven to 425 degrees F.
3. Grease two rimmed baking sheets.
4. Spread wings in a single layer on the baking sheets.
5. Roast wings until very crisp, about 45 minutes.
6. Serve with salsa for dipping.

Bacon Taco Chicken Wings

Ingredients:

3 lbs. chicken wings, split at the joints, tips removed
3 tbsps. taco seasoning
1 package bacon
Salsa for dipping

Directions:

1. Toss the wings with the taco seasoning.
2. Preheat oven to 425 degrees F.
3. Grease two rimmed baking sheets.
4. Wrap each wing in a strip of bacon.
5. Spread wings in a single layer on the baking sheets.
6. Roast wings until very crisp, about 45 minutes.
7. Serve with salsa for dipping.

Mole Chicken Wings

Ingredients:

3 lbs. chicken wings, split at the joints, tips removed
Salt and pepper to taste
1/3 cup mole sauce
Juice of 2 oranges
2 tbsps. honey
1/4 cup water

Directions:

1. Season the wings with salt and pepper.
2. Preheat oven to 425 degrees F.
3. Grease two rimmed baking sheets.
4. Spread wings in a single layer on the baking sheets.
5. Roast wings until very crisp, about 45 minutes.
6. In a small saucepan, heat the mole sauce, orange juice, honey and water.
7. Toss with the wings and serve!

Lemon Garlic Chicken Wings

Ingredients:

3 lbs. chicken wings, split at the joints, tips removed
Salt to taste
1 1/2 tsps. paprika
3 tbsps. lemon juice
3 tbsps. sliced garlic
1 tsp. lemon zest

Directions:

1. Mix salt and paprika and toss with the wings.
2. Preheat oven to 425 degrees F.
3. Grease two rimmed baking sheets.
4. Spread wings in a single layer on the baking sheets.
5. Roast wings for about 35 minutes.
6. Sprinkle with lemon juice, garlic and lemon zest.
7. Roast 10 minutes more.
8. Serve and enjoy!

Aïoli Chicken Wings

Ingredients:

3 lbs. chicken wings, split at the joints, tips removed
Salt and pepper to taste
1/2 cup mayonnaise
1 garlic clove, finely grated
1 tbsp. olive oil
1 tbsp. lemon juice

Directions:

1. Season the wings with salt and pepper.
2. Preheat oven to 425 degrees F.
3. Grease two rimmed baking sheets.
4. Spread wings in a single layer on the baking sheets.
5. Roast wings until very crisp, about 45 minutes.
6. Whisk together mayonnaise, garlic, olive oil and lemon juice for a dipping sauce.
7. Serve with the wings.
8. Enjoy!

Pesto Wings

Ingredients:

3 lbs. chicken wings, split at the joints, tips removed
Salt and pepper
1/2 cup pesto
1/4 cup grated Parmesan

Directions:

1. Season the wings with salt and pepper.
2. Preheat oven to 425 degrees F.
3. Grease two rimmed baking sheets.
4. Spread wings in a single layer on the baking sheets.
5. Roast wings until very crisp, about 45 minutes.
6. Toss wings with pesto and grated Parmesan.
7. Serve and enjoy!

Pizza Wings

Ingredients:

3 lbs. chicken wings, split at the joints, tips removed
Salt to taste
2 tsps. dried oregano
1/4 cup sliced pepperoni
1/2 cup sliced onion
Mozzarella cheese
Marinara sauce for dipping

Directions:

1. Toss the wings with salt and oregano.
2. Preheat oven to 425 degrees F.
3. Grease two rimmed baking sheets.
4. Spread wings in a single layer on the baking sheets.
5. Roast wings for 30 minutes.
6. Spread pepperoni and onion the baking sheets with the wings.
7. Roast wings for 15 more minutes.
8. Toss with shredded mozzarella
9. Serve with marinara sauce.
10. Enjoy!

Popcorn Chicken Wings

Ingredients:

3 pounds chicken wings, split at the joints, tips removed
8 cups white cheddar popcorn
2 tsps. chipotle chile powder
Flour for dredging
3 eggs, beaten
Ranch dressing for dipping

Directions:

1. Preheat oven to 425 degrees F.
2. Grease two rimmed baking sheets.
3. Finely grind popcorn and chipotle chile powder in a food processor.
4. In separate bowls, put flour, then egg, then popcorn mixture.
5. Dredge the wings first in flour, then dip in eggs and then coat in the ground popcorn mixture.
6. Spread wings out on pans.
7. Roast in preheated oven, turning once, until crisp, 45 minutes.
8. Serve with ranch dip and enjoy!

Carolina Wings

Ingredients:

1 pounds chicken wings, split at the joints, tips removed
1 tbsp. salt
1 tbsp. black pepper
1/4 cup ketchup
1/2 cup red wine vinegar
1/4 tsp. red chili flakes
1 tbsp. adobo sauce
1 tsp. dry mustard
2 tsps. granulated garlic
1 tsp. sugar

Directions:

1. Preheat the oven to 350 degrees F.
2. Season the wings with salt and pepper.
3. Arrange the chicken wings on a baking sheet in a single layer.
4. Put in the preheated oven and cook for 45 minutes.
5. Remove the wings from the oven to a bowl and allow to cool.
6. Combine the remaining ingredients in a bowl.
7. Toss with the wings and enjoy!

Memphis Dry-Rub Wings

Ingredients:

1 pounds chicken wings, split at the joints, tips removed
1/8 cup unrefined evaporated cane sugar
1/8 cup golden or light brown sugar
1/3 cup kosher salt or medium fine sea salt
2 tsp sweet Hungarian paprika
2 tsp. chili powder
2 tsp. granulated onion
2 tsp. ground mustard
1/3 tbsp. granulated garlic
3/4 tsp. dried thyme
3/4 tsp. dried oregano
3/4 tsp. fresh ground black pepper
3/4 tsp. celery salt
3/4 tsp. ground ginger
1/3 tsp. ground coriander
1/3 tsp. ground cayenne
Canola oil spray
1 large plastic resealable bag

Directions:

1. In large bowl mix together all ingredients except the wings.
2. Set aside.
3. Rinse wings in cold water and dry with paper towel.
4. Place wings in large plastic resealable bag and add 1/3 cup of rub.
5. Set remaining rub aside.
6. Seal bag and shake to evenly coat wings.
7. Place bag on lipped sheet pan or cookie sheet and refrigerate for 2 hours to overnight.
8. Drain liquid from bag.
9. Add 2 more tbsps. rub.
10. Seal and shake to evenly coat wings.
11. Set aside.
12. Spray grill grates with canola oil.

13. Set grill to medium heat (250-275 degrees F) and prepare for indirect cooking.
14. When grill is hot, using tongs, place wings on cool side of grill and cook over indirect heat for 1 hour.
15. Flip wings and lightly spray wings with canola oil.
16. Dust wings very lightly with rub and cook for 1 hour or until internal temperature is at least 165 degrees F.
17. Serve and enjoy!

Kentucky Barbecue Chicken Wings

Ingredients:

3 pounds chicken wings, split at the joints, tips removed
1 3/4 cups water
1 cup plus 2 tbsps. catsup
1/4 cup plus 2 tbsps. Worcestershire sauce
1 tsp. paprika
1 tsp. dry mustard
3/4 tsp. garlic salt
3/4 tsp. onion powder
1 1/2 tsps. red pepper
3/4 tsp. pepper

Directions:

1. Preheat oven to 425 degrees F.
2. Grease two rimmed baking sheets.
3. Spread wings in a single layer on the baking sheets.
4. Roast wings crisp, about 35 minutes.
5. Combine all ingredients except wings in a large saucepan, mixing well.
6. Bring to a boil.
7. Reduce heat to medium.
8. Cook, uncovered, 20 minutes, stirring occasionally.
9. Toss with the wings and enjoy!

Honey BBQ Chicken Wings

Ingredients:

3 pounds chicken wings, split at the joints, tips removed
1/2 cup reduced-sodium soy sauce
1/2 cup barbecue sauce
1/2 cup honey
1 cup all-purpose flour
2 tsps. salt
2 tsps. paprika
1/4 tsp. pepper
Oil for deep-fat frying

Directions:

1. In a small saucepan, combine the soy sauce, barbecue sauce and honey.
2. Bring to a boil.
3. Cook until liquid is reduced to about 1 cup.
4. Meanwhile, in a large resealable plastic bag, combine the flour, salt, paprika and pepper.
5. Add wings a few at a time, and shake to coat.
6. In a deep fryer or skillet, heat oil to 375 degrees F.
7. Fry wings, a few at a time, for 3-4 minutes on each side or until no longer pink.
8. Drain on paper towels.
9. Transfer wings to a large bowl.
10. Add sauce and toss to coat.
11. Serve and enjoy!

Tandoori Chicken Wings

Ingredients:

3 pounds chicken wings, split at the joints, tips removed
1/2 cup tandoori paste
1/2 cup Greek yogurt

Directions:

1. Marinate the wings in tandoori paste and Greek yogurt for 30 minutes.
2. Grill wings on grill over medium heat, turning, until cooked through, 15 to 20 minutes.
3. Serve and enjoy!

Hawaiian Chicken Wings

Ingredients:

3 pounds chicken wings, split at the joints, tips removed
1 1/2 cups pineapple chunks
1 tbsp. oyster sauce
1 tbsp. honey
Salt to taste
1 tbsp. vegetable oil

Directions:

1. Purée pineapple chunks, oyster sauce and honey.
2. Toss the wings with salt and vegetable oil.
3. Grill wings on grill over medium heat, turning, until cooked through, 15 to 20 minutes.
4. Brush the wings with the sauce in the last 5 minutes.
5. Serve and enjoy!

Blackened Chicken Wings

Ingredients:

3 pounds chicken wings, split at the joints, tips removed
1 1/2 tsps. Cajun seasoning
1 1/2 tsps. paprika
1 1/2 tsps. cayenne
1 1/2 tsps. dried oregano
1 1/2 tsps. thyme
kosher salt and pepper to taste.

Directions:

1. Mix all the ingredients together except the wings.
2. Toss spice mixture with the wings.
3. Grill wings on grill over medium heat, turning, until cooked through, 15 to 20 minutes.
4. Serve and enjoy!

Tequila Lime Chicken Wings

3 pounds chicken wings, split at the joints, tips removed
1/4 cup tequila
1/4 cup lime juice
2 tbsps. agave nectar
2 tbsps. olive oil
salt and pepper to taste,

Directions:

1. Mix all the ingredients together except the wings.
2. Marinate the wings in the mixture for two hours.
3. Grill wings on grill over medium heat, turning, until cooked through, 15 to 20 minutes.
4. Serve and enjoy!

Rice Crispy Wings

Ingredients:

1 lb. chicken wing sections
1 tsp. kosher salt
1/2 tsp. freshly ground black pepper
1/4 tsp. cayenne pepper
1/2 cup stone-ground rice flour
2 cups vegetable oil for frying, or as needed

Directions:

1. Place split chicken wings into a mixing bowl.
2. Sprinkle with salt, black pepper, and cayenne pepper.
3. Toss to evenly coat pieces.
4. Cover with plastic wrap and refrigerate for at least 2 hours or overnight.
5. Place rice flour in a shallow dish. Dredge chicken wing pieces in small batches in the flour and transfer to a plate.
6. Arrange pieces so there is some space between them; allow wings to sit out for 15 minutes before frying.
7. Line a baking sheet with paper towels; place a draining rack on the towels.
8. Heat oil in a deep-fryer or large saucepan to 375 degrees F (190 degrees C). Transfer wings to oil; fry until inside is crispy and golden brown and chicken is cooked through, 10 to 12 minutes. An instant-read thermometer inserted near the bone should read 165 degrees F (74 degrees C).
9. Remove wings from oil with a slotted spoon and drain on a rack placed over paper towels.

Australian Deep Fried Chicken Wings

Ingredients:

8 chicken wings
4 tbsps. soy sauce
3 tbsps. oyster sauce
3 tbsps. sweet sherry
Salt and pepper to taste
1/2 cup all-purpose flour
1/2 cup corn flour
1 quart oil for deep frying

Directions:

1. To Marinate: Place the chicken wings in a large nonporous glass dish or bowl.
2. In a small bowl mix the soy sauce, oyster sauce, sherry, salt and pepper and pour mixture over chicken; turn to coat.
3. Cover dish and refrigerate to marinate for 12 to 24 hours.
4. Remove chicken from marinade, disposing of any remaining marinade.
5. Mix all-purpose flour with corn flour in a shallow dish or bowl and toss wings in flour mixture until well coated.
6. Heat oil in a deep skillet or deep fryer and deep fry wings until crispy and cooked through (juices run clear).
7. Drain on paper towels and serve.

Caesar Grilled Chicken Wings

Ingredients:

1 (8 oz.) bottle Caesar salad dressing
1/4 cup freshly grated Parmesan cheese
3 lbs. chicken wings
1 tbsp. lemon pepper

Directions:

1. Combine Caesar dressing and Parmesan cheese in a bowl.
2. Place wings in a large resealable plastic bag; pour in dressing-cheese marinade. Seal bag; toss to coat and refrigerate at least 4 hours.
3. Preheat grill for medium heat (300 to 350 degrees F, 150 to 175 degrees C), and lightly oil the grate.
4. Remove wings from bag; discard marinade. Heavily sprinkle all sides of wings with lemon pepper.
5. Place wings on grill.
6. Cook, covered, turning several times, until cooked through and internal temperature reaches 165 degrees F (75 degrees C); 20 to 30 minutes. Transfer wings to a platter.

Tequila Sunrise Chicken Wings

Ingredients:

1 (10 oz.) jar prepared jalapeno pepper jelly
1 cup orange juice
1 cup tequila
2 lbs. chicken wings
1/2 gallon vegetable oil for frying
1/2 cup butter
1/4 cup Thai-style chili sauce

Directions:

1. Whisk jalapeno pepper jelly, orange juice, and tequila together in a bowl until smooth; pour into a large resealable plastic bag.
2. Add chicken wings, coat with the marinade, squeeze to remove excess air, and seal the bag. Marinate in the refrigerator 4 hours to overnight.
3. Heat oil in a deep-fryer or large saucepan to 375 degrees F (190 degrees C).
4. Remove chicken wings from the marinade and shake to remove excess moisture. Blot wings dry with paper towel. Discard the remaining marinade.
5. Fry chicken wings in batches in hot oil until golden brown on the outside and no longer pink on the inside, 10 to 15 minutes per batch.
6. Drain on a wire baking rack.
7. Melt butter in a saucepan over medium heat.
8. Stir chili sauce into the melted butter until the color is consistent; pour into a large stainless steel bowl.
9. Add chicken wings and toss to coat in the sauce.

Jalapeno Apple Hot Wings

Ingredients:

1 tsp. vegetable oil
2 jalapeno peppers, seeded and finely chopped
2 cloves garlic, minced
1/2 tsp. ground cumin
1/2 tsp. red pepper flakes
1 pinch ground ginger
2 cups buttermilk
4 1/2 lbs. chicken wings, tips discarded
1 tbsp. olive oil
2 1/4 tsps. salt, divided
1/2 tsp. ground black pepper
1/2 (12 fluid oz.) can frozen apple juice concentrate
1/3 cup lemon juice
1/4 cup honey
1 tbsp. hot pepper sauce
1 tbsp. Worcestershire sauce

Directions:

1. Heat vegetable oil in a skillet over medium-high heat. Saute jalapeno peppers, garlic, cumin, and red pepper flakes in hot oil until vegetables are tender and fragrant, about 5 minutes; cool completely.
2. Stir buttermilk and cooled jalapeno mixture together in a large glass or ceramic bowl; add chicken wings and stir to coat wings completely.
3. Cover the bowl with plastic wrap and refrigerate for at least 8 hours or overnight.
4. Drain chicken and discard buttermilk mixture.
5. Set oven rack about 6 inches from the heat source and preheat the oven's broiler.
6. Toss chicken wings with olive oil, 2 tsps. salt, and black pepper in a large bowl.
7. Spread wings out in an even layer on a baking sheet.
8. Cook chicken in the preheated oven, turning once, until almost cooked through, 20 to 25 minutes.

9. Remove from oven.
10. Whisk apple juice concentrate, lemon juice, honey, hot pepper sauce, Worcestershire sauce, and remaining 1/4 tsp. salt together in a large saucepan; bring to a boil and cook until mixture is reduced by half and syrupy, about 20 minutes.
11. Brush 1/4 cup the apple juice sauce on the chicken wings. Return wings to oven and continue cooking for 1 to 2 minutes.
12. Brush wings again with 1/4 cup apple juice sauce, turn wings, and brush wings with another 1/4 cup apple juice sauce.
13. erve with remaining apple juice sauce.

Waffle Stuffed Chicken Wings

Ingredients:

2 cups Belgian waffle mix
1 1/2 cups water
1/3 cup vegetable oil
Cooking spray
1 lb. chicken wings with skin
1 cup maple syrup
1/8 tsp. cayenne pepper

Directions:

1. Combine waffle mix, water, and vegetable oil in a large bowl; stir until no lumps remain. Let stand until thickened, 4 to 5 minutes.
2. Heat a Belgian waffle iron according to manufacturers' instructions.
3. Grease with cooking spray.
4. Pour 1/4 of the waffle batter into the iron; close and cook until golden brown, about 5 minutes.
5. Repeat with remaining batter. Cool waffles on a wire rack.
6. Preheat oven to 400 degrees F (200 degrees C).
7. Cut waffles into small pieces. Stuff pieces between the meat and skin of the chicken wings.
8. Place chicken wings on a baking sheet.
9. Bake in the preheated oven until wings are golden brown and crisp, 45 to 50 minutes. Let cool.
10. Bring maple syrup to a simmer in a small saucepan over medium-low heat.
11. Stir in cayenne pepper. Simmer until thickened to a glaze, about 10 minutes.
12. Remove from heat.
13. Combine cooled chicken wings and maple glaze in a large bowl; toss until coated.

Garlic and Parmesan Chicken Wings

Ingredients:

Cooking spray
3 quarts cold water
1/3 cup balsamic vinegar
1/4 cup salt
1 bay leaf
1 tsp. dried thyme
1 tsp. dried oregano
1 tsp. dried rosemary
8 cloves garlic, minced
1 pinch salt
3 tbsps. olive oil, or as needed
1 tbsp. freshly ground black pepper
2 tsps. red pepper flakes, or to taste
4 lbs. chicken wings, separated at joints, tips discarded
2 tbsps. fine bread crumbs
1 cup finely grated Parmigiano-Reggiano cheese, divided

Directions:

1. Preheat an oven to 450 degrees F (230 degrees C). Line a baking sheet with aluminum foil and coat foil with cooking spray.
2. Combine water, vinegar, 1/4 cup salt, bay leaf, thyme, oregano, and rosemary in a large stockpot and bring to a boil.
3. Add chicken wings, return to a boil, and cook for 15 minutes.
4. Remove chicken wings with a slotted spoon to a cooling rack and allow to dry for 15 minutes.
5. Mash garlic and a pinch of salt together in a mortar and pestle until smooth.
6. Combine mashed garlic, olive oil, black pepper, and red pepper flakes in a large bowl.
7. Add chicken wings and bread crumbs; toss to coat.

8. Sprinkle with 1/2 cup Parmigiano-Reggiano cheese. Transfer to the prepared baking sheet and sprinkle with remaining 1/2 cup Parmigiano-Reggiano cheese.
9. Bake in the preheated oven until browned, 20 to 25 miutes.

Thousand Island Wings

Ingredients:

1 (8 fluid oz.) bottle Thousand Island salad dressing
1 (8 oz.) jar apricot jam
1 (1 oz.) package dry onion soup mix
6 large chicken wings

Directions:

1. Preheat oven to 350 degrees F (175 degrees C).
2. Stir Thousand Island salad dressing, apricot jam, and onion soup mix together in a large bowl until smooth.
3. Arrange chicken wings into a baking dish; pour the sauce over the wings.
4. Cover dish with aluminum foil.
5. Bake the chicken in the preheated oven for 30 minutes.
6. Remove foil and continue baking until no longer pink at the bone and the juices run clear, about 30 minutes more.

About the Author

Laura Sommers is **The Recipe Lady!**

She is a loving wife and mother who lives on a small farm in Baltimore County, Maryland and has a passion for all things domestic especially when it comes to saving money. She has a profitable eBay business and is a couponing addict. Follow her tips and tricks to learn how to make delicious meals on a budget, save money or to learn the latest life hack!

Visit her Amazon Author Page to see her latest books:

amazon.com/author/laurasommers

Visit the Recipe Lady's blog for even more great recipes:

http://the-recipe-lady.blogspot.com/

Follow the Recipe Lady on **Pinterest**:

http://pinterest.com/therecipelady1

Follow the Recipe Lady on **Facebook**:

https://www.facebook.com/therecipegirl/

If you enjoyed this book, please leave a review. It really helps me support my family. Thank you!

Other Books by Laura Sommers

- **Party Dip Recipes for the Big Game**
- **50 Super Awesome Salsa Recipes!**
- **Super Summer Barbecue and Pool Party Picnic Salad Recipes!**
- **50 Super Awesome Coleslaw and Potato Salad Recipes**
- **Homemade Salad Dressing Recipes from Scratch!**
- **50 Super Awesome Pasta Salad Recipes!**
- **50 Delicious Homemade Ice Cream Recipes**